WHAT WOULD HAPPEN IF...

WE STOPPED USING CARS?

Written by Izzi Howell

Illustrated by Paula Bossio

WORLD BOOK

www.worldbook.com

READING TIPS

This book asks readers to ponder the question *what would happen if we stopped using cars?* Readers will discover how heavy car use is leading to environmental problems and energy challenges. They will contemplate a world without cars, as well as consider other transportation solutions. Use these tips to help readers consider the ripple effects of certain actions and events.

Before Reading

Explain to readers that this book uses cause and effect to show how cars affect our everyday lives, our health, the environment, and our planet's resources. Cause and effect can help us think about why things happen the way they do. It can also help us think about what might happen in the future because of our actions and choices today. Encourage readers to be on the lookout for examples of a cause and effect structure as they explore what would happen if we stopped using cars.

During Reading

Discuss with readers how some actions and events have multiple causes and others have multiple effects. Explain that it can be tricky to keep all the if/then scenarios straight in our minds, so it can be helpful to create a visual guide. Encourage readers to draw and add notes to their own cause and effect maps like those found on pages 14-15 and 24-25.

After Reading

After finishing the book, discuss with readers how their understandings and opinions of cars and their effect on our planet and the environment have changed. Additionally, you can have readers respond to the comprehension questions included on page 46 and complete the Chain of Events activity on page 47 to further extend the learning.

Visit www.worldbook.com/resources for additional, free educational materials.

There is a glossary of terms on pages 44–45. Terms defined in the glossary are in boldface type that **looks like this** on their first appearance on any spread (two facing pages).

Contents

A car crisis?

Cars are probably the most important form of transportation for the majority of people around the world. Since their invention in the late 1800's, cars have revolutionized the way we live our lives. They influence where and how we build towns and cities, how businesses operate, and how people move around their local area and beyond.

DID YOU KNOW?

There's approximately one car for every eight people on Earth!

The fastest speed recorded by a car was an incredible 763 mph (1,228 kph), but don't try that at home!

The average car is made up of around 30,000 individual parts.

Most cars are parked for 96 percent of the time!

The most expensive car ever sold cost $135 million.

When cars first came on the market, they were far too pricey for most people. Over time, the price of cars has come down dramatically, and they have become an essential part of everyday life in many countries. As a result, the number of cars on the road worldwide has rocketed. Heavy car use by so many people is leading to many environmental problems, including pollution and **global warming.**

People who live in **remote** areas, such as this part of Western Australia, would struggle to work, get groceries, or access health care without cars.

THINK ABOUT IT!

Does your family own a car? What do you use it for? How would your lives change if you couldn't use it anymore?

It's becoming increasingly clear that we can't continue to use cars in the same way forever—our planet simply can't take it! We are also on track to run out of **fossil fuels** in the next hundred years or so, which would mean no more gasoline to power traditional cars. After more than a century dominated by cars, what would our world look like in the future if we stopped using cars altogether?

Driving through time

Did you know that cars have been around for less than 150 years? This makes them younger than flushable toilets, elevators, and telephones!

The first gasoline-powered cars were developed and built in Europe in the 1880's. These early machines were built by hand, and so they came at a massive cost. Only the wealthiest people in society could afford to buy a car.

This car was built in the mid-1890's in Germany. Passengers had to bring an umbrella if it was raining!

Who needs a car anyway?! I'm just as fast!

FUN FACT!
Some of the first cars couldn't move much faster than a fast walking pace, even at their top speed!

Just ... a ... little ... bumpy!

After 1900, the center of the car **industry** moved from Europe to the United States, when early car pioneers like Henry Ford developed ways of mass-producing cars. Using **assembly lines** hugely sped up the process, which allowed prices to drop. As cars became more affordable, more and more people started to buy them.

In the 1960's, more countries began developing their car industries, including Japan, West Germany, Italy, and France. Over the next few decades, car ownership grew around the world.

Nowadays, cars are the main way of getting around in many places. It's hard to imagine life without them, and in some areas, it's truly almost impossible to live without one!

DRIVING THROUGH TIME

Car ownership is more common in more economically developed countries. Here, even people with "average" jobs usually have disposable income and can afford to buy and run a car. In less economically developed areas, cars are often a luxury item.

However, car ownership isn't always a question of wealth. Some cities and countries prioritize public transportation and invest in regular services that take people wherever they need to go. In these areas, people don't need to depend on personal cars, and so many choose not to own one. There is also an increasing number of people who have decided not to own a car for environmental reasons.

14 四ツ谷線 for Har
Yamanote Line

Every day, nearly 6 million people use the subway system in Tokyo, Japan. Just imagine if all those people drove instead!

In the past few decades, electric and **hybrid** cars have become much more widespread. Electric cars use electric motors that run on energy stored in a rechargeable battery. They don't produce any exhaust **emissions** and are much quieter than traditional cars. However, it takes much longer to recharge their batteries than it does to fill a traditional car with gasoline, which can make it tricky to travel large distances.

People with electric cars often install charging points outside their home, so that they can easily recharge their car's battery.

Hybrid cars have traditional engines and electric motors. They offer the advantages of both types of vehicles, but also some of the disadvantages (like exhaust emissions ... ahem, ahem!).

FUN FACT!

The first electric car was actually created around the same time as gasoline-powered cars, but they didn't catch on at the time!

We're so ahead of our time!

9

The cost of cars

Let's face it—cars are superconvenient and can make everyday life much easier! However, it's important to look beyond those pluses and see the full picture. Cars have many flaws, including their massive negative impact on the environment, the risk to drivers and **pedestrians** alike, and their irritating noise pollution, to name just a few!

Up until recently, all cars were powered by gasoline or diesel, which come from **fossil fuels.** These fuels are burned inside a car's engine to create energy. Burning these fuels also releases certain gases, which are emitted from the car through its exhaust pipe.

WHAT IS RELEASED IN A CAR'S EXHAUST?

PARTICULATE MATTER
Fancy name, but these are just tiny pieces of dirt, dust, and soot that float in the air. If they are breathed in, they can cause health problems.

CARBON DIOXIDE
This **greenhouse gas** heavily contributes to the **greenhouse effect** and **global warming** (read on for more information).

CARBON MONOXIDE
Warning! This invisible, odorless gas is very **toxic** to humans!

NITROGEN OXIDE
This gas can create a thick type of air pollution called **smog** when it reacts with other chemicals in the air.

SULFUR DIOXIDE
This poisonous gas can also create smog.

Where are you?

Areas with heavy traffic experience high levels of air pollution. People who live there breathe in these nasty gases day after day, which leads to increased rates of breathing problems, lung cancer, heart diseases, and many other health problems.

In heavily polluted cities, some people wear masks to protect them from breathing in harmful gases.

Car exhaust also contributes greatly to global warming. This is because it contains high levels of carbon dioxide—a greenhouse gas that gathers in Earth's **atmosphere.** Greenhouse gases trap heat from the sun close to Earth, which makes it warmer on the surface. This change in temperature is linked to extreme weather and **habitat** destruction, and it's putting the lives of many animals and plants at risk.

Polar ice is melting because of global warming, leaving such animals as polar bears without a place to hunt or shelter.

Cars themselves also pose a significant risk to anyone around them, inside or outside the car. A car crash can injure, or even kill, the driver, passengers, nearby **pedestrians,** or other road users, including those on bikes or in other cars. Speeding, improper use of seat belts and infant car seats, driving while distracted (for example, while checking your phone!), and unsafe roads all increase the risk of an accident.

People aren't the only victims of car crashes. Many animals that live near roads are hit and killed by cars while they are trying to cross to the other side. This is a particular problem on major highways that go through the countryside.

DID YOU KNOW?

Around 1.3 million people die in road traffic accidents every year. They are the leading cause of death for children and young people.

The construction of roads through the countryside also damages many natural **habitats.** Trees and plants that animals depend on for food and shelter are chopped down. Valuable sources of drinking water for animals, such as streams and lakes, are blocked up or paved over to create wider roads to accommodate more cars.

Vroom! Beep-beep! If you live anywhere near a road, you're probably familiar with the racket produced by cars. In small quantities, this noise is just annoying, but busy traffic can be so loud that it is considered a type of noise pollution. Noise pollution can lead to sleeping problems and even increased rates of heart disease.

Noise pollution also disrupts animal behavior. Animals can't communicate properly if they can't hear each other!

What?

Croak, croak!

Many modern towns and cities were not built with **pedestrians** or public transportation in mind. Such important services as schools, hospitals, and grocery stores are far away from residential areas. With poor or no public transit connections, and sometimes not even sidewalks to walk along, people in these areas are entirely dependent on cars.

Life in these places is convenient for people who have cars, but extremely challenging for those who don't. People who can't afford a car, are too young or old to drive, or are disabled find it very hard to get around and experience many difficulties. Let's take a look …

What are some of the challenges of life without a car in a car-dependent area?

CHILD

It may be difficult or impossible to reach friends' homes in certain areas or do activities and hobbies located far from public transportation routes.

Unreliable public transportation makes it harder to arrive at school on time.

Children miss out on socializing and developing their interests outside of school.

Children may miss valuable classes and tests.

Without the full amount of time in school, children may not reach their potential.

I guess I'll practice swimming here!

ADULT

Adults can only do jobs that are **accessible** on foot or public transportation.

They may be forced to do a job that doesn't pay well or isn't part of their career plan, since they have no other alternative.

Public transit delays and cancellations make it hard to arrive at work on time.

In extreme cases, adults may end up being fired for lateness.

THINK ABOUT IT!

People who can't afford a car often find it challenging to earn enough money to buy one. Why do you think that is? Use the information on this page to help you.

15

Farewell cars?

The end of traditional **fossil fuel-**powered cars is drawing closer and closer! Scientists predict that we only have enough oil to last us another 50 years at most. And once oil is gone, we won't be able to make any more gasoline or diesel to power cars.

If we want to keep the climate crisis from getting worse, we need to stop using such machines as oil rigs to extract fossil fuels and leave them in the ground permanently!

Even if we had enough fossil fuels to last us forever, we would still have the massive problem that we really shouldn't be using any more of them! Scientists have advised people to stop **extracting** and burning fossil fuels due to the extreme climate crisis they create. If we don't get **global warming** under control soon, we may damage our planet beyond repair. Stopping the use of all cars would immediately reduce our use of fossil fuels by a huge amount.

DID YOU KNOW?

If global warming is allowed to continue, sea levels are expected to have risen by a foot (30 cm) by 2050.

Extreme heat and periods of **drought** linked to **climate change** are putting many crops at risk. Many people could go hungry as a result.

Hi! I'm Myles Allen, a British scientist who studies climate change. I'm passionate about the need to reduce our **greenhouse gas emissions** to "net zero." This means that the amount of greenhouse gases we release is balanced exactly by the amount we remove from our **atmosphere**. The easiest way of reaching net zero is to dramatically cut our greenhouse gas emissions, for example, by stopping the use of all traditional cars. It's now or never if we want to protect our planet from a climate crisis!

17

But wait ... what about electric cars? Aren't they an obvious solution to our **fossil fuel** problem? Well, yes and no! While electric cars don't run directly on fossil fuels or emit harmful gases, they aren't a perfect environmentally friendly solution.

Fossil fuel-powered cars can't be converted to run on electricity, so if we switched to electric cars, every car on Earth would need to be replaced. This would require a huge number of resources, from metal for the car exterior and minerals for the car's battery to rubber for the tires and plastic for the car interior.

Extracting and processing these resources and then turning them into cars requires lots of power, which almost always comes from burning fossil fuels. Using our existing fossil fuel-powered cars until the end of their lives would actually be a better choice for the environment than buying brand-new electric cars.

DID YOU KNOW?

Building a new electric car generates about 80 percent more **emissions** than building a new fossil fuel-powered car.

This is a cobalt mine in the mountains of Morocco. Cobalt is one of the minerals used to create batteries for electric cars. Mines like this destroy and pollute wild areas that are home to many animals and plants.

But that's not the end of the story. Electric cars need to be charged with electricity, and where does that electricity usually come from? That's right—from burning fossil fuels! Many countries still burn coal, oil, and natural gas to generate their country's electricity supply, which means that charging your electric car isn't always quite as green as you might think.

A coal power plant like this might be generating the electricity used to power an "environmentally friendly" electric car!

THINK ABOUT IT!

Electric cars are expensive. Why would this be a problem if the choice was made to replace all cars with electric vehicles?

So, instead of trying to replace fossil fuel-powered cars with electric cars, what would happen if we stopped using personal cars altogether? Let's take a look!

A cleaner planet

If we all stopped using cars, it would make a big difference to the environment. Almost immediately, we'd notice big changes in the levels of air pollution and **emissions.**

The end of cars would also mean the end of almost all vehicle exhaust emissions (other than those from buses and other public transit vehicles). Without such **toxic** gases as carbon monoxide or sulfur dioxide being pumped out all day, every day, air quality would drastically improve around roads. We'd also have less **smog** in cities, which would improve visibility.

In the short term, people with breathing problems, such as asthma, would probably enjoy fewer symptoms. In the long term, cases of lung disease, heart disease, and certain cancers would probably fall in areas that had once experienced high levels of pollution from traffic. Woo-hoo!

I'm feeling SO much better!

We've actually already had a sneak peek at what a world without cars might look like. During the COVID-19 pandemic, car use dropped dramatically around the world during lockdowns, and within a few weeks, the skies were clearer, the air was cleaner, and people experienced many fewer breathing issues in particularly polluted areas. Just imagine how much the world would change if we stopped using cars forever!

FUN FACT!

During the COVID-19 lockdown in India, the Himalaya mountains became visible from over 100 miles (160 kilometers) away for the first time in 30 years due to the drop in air pollution!

A CLEANER PLANET

The end of cars wouldn't just benefit human health—the health of our planet would also greatly improve! As we've already seen, the **carbon dioxide** in car exhaust is one of the biggest contributors to the **greenhouse effect,** which leads to **global warming** and **climate change.** Stopping nearly all vehicle **emissions** would keep our planet from plunging deeper into a climate crisis.

Bangladesh and many other parts of the world are already experiencing serious flooding because of extreme weather linked to climate change. These events would become less frequent if we reduced **greenhouse gas** emissions.

However, the end of cars wouldn't be the end of global warming. We'd still need to deal with the emissions from other sources, such as **fossil fuel** power plants and livestock farming. We'd also need to work on removing carbon dioxide from our **atmosphere** if we want to reverse the problem. This could be through modern carbon capture technology or more traditional techniques, such as planting trees!

Trees absorb and store carbon as they grow, which makes them the perfect natural carbon store!

Hi! I'm Arup SenGupta, a chemist and engineer with a particular interest in water. My team and I have come up with a new way to capture carbon dioxide from the atmosphere and store it in seawater. Removing carbon dioxide would help reduce the greenhouse effect and its effects on our planet. Stopping the use of cars would be a great step in the right direction, but without carbon capture technology to remove excess carbon, we won't see major improvements in climate change anytime soon.

Guess the secret ingredient!

23

How would the environment improve if we stopped using cars?

No more cars means no more **greenhouse gases** or **toxic** fumes released by the 1 billion cars currently on Earth.

Air pollution would quickly decrease, particularly around busy highways and in crowded cities.

Preexisting breathing problems would get better within a few weeks or months. In the long run, rates of more serious diseases, such as cancer and heart disease, would decrease in previously polluted areas.

Smog would become rarer, and visibility would improve in cities.

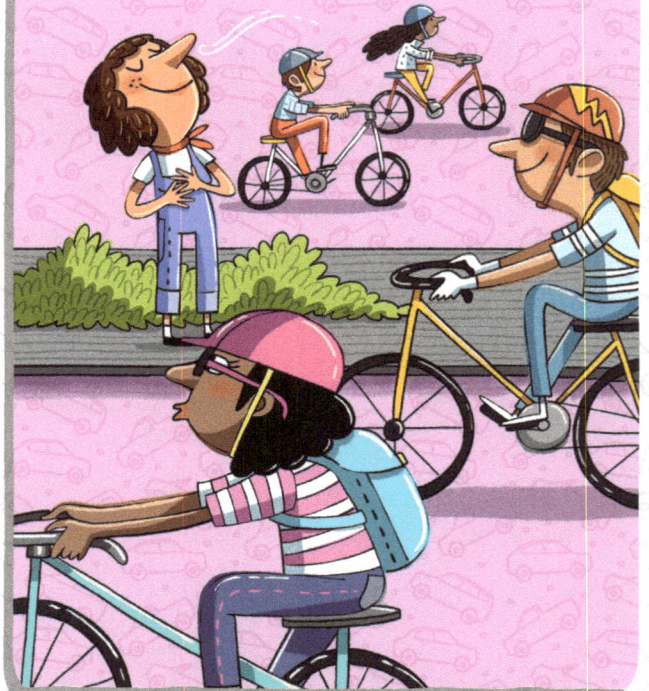

Overall **carbon dioxide emissions** would be greatly reduced. **Global warming** would stop getting worse and would stabilize at current levels.

However, global warming wouldn't go away altogether unless we removed all the excess carbon dioxide remaining in our **atmosphere**. We could do this through carbon storage techniques.

By enforcing an overall end to the use of all cars and cleaning up our atmosphere, we could reverse global warming and eventually get temperatures back to what they were a few hundred years ago.

THINK ABOUT IT

Can you imagine a world without global warming? What would be the biggest positive changes?

Our changing society

Although ending the use of cars would have nothing but a positive impact on the environment, it would have a much more complicated effect on everyday life. Cars are a lifeline for many people around the world. Without cars, they wouldn't be able to work, attend school, buy groceries, seek medical attention, or do countless other important tasks.

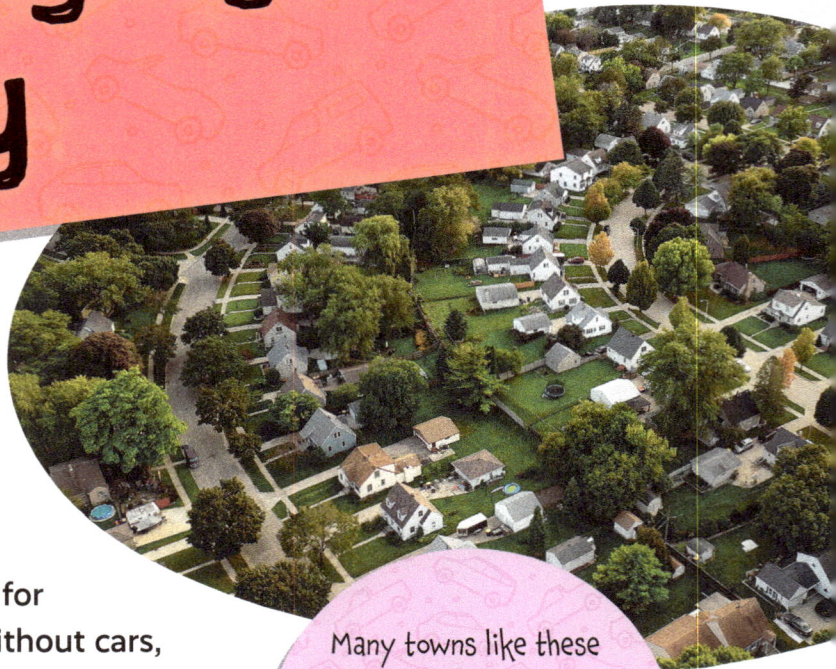

Many towns like these are full of houses but little else! You have to travel to reach essential services, and for that, you need a car!

THINK ABOUT IT

Why do you think cars are so important in rural communities? Why is it hard to set up public transportation services in these areas?

Suddenly restricting cars from areas without good public transportation or **rural** communities would create chaos. With no alternatives to cars already in place, people would struggle to live their lives as usual. They'd essentially be trapped in their homes without access to anything they need!

As we've seen before, this would lead to many issues. In the short run, people might end up going hungry because they couldn't regularly visit the supermarket or miss out on urgent medical appointments they need to stay healthy. In the long run, children might miss out on their education, which would limit their options in life. Adults would find it hard to get a job and regularly make it to work. Without a good, regular income, they could end up living in poverty.

We've got to get up early to make it to school on time!

So what could we do to solve this problem? Turn the page to find out!

OUR CHANGING SOCIETY

To begin with, we'd need massive worldwide investment in public transportation. Buses would probably be the simplest short-term solution, since they could drive along existing roads. They could even be powered by electricity for an added environmental boost!

Governments could also offer financial assistance to help more people buy their own bikes or electric bikes, which are a great solution for shorter journeys. Electric bikes provide a helpful boost on steep hills or if you are carrying groceries (or your kids!) in a bike trailer!

Other forms of public transportation, such as trains and trams, would take much longer to set up, as new train lines, stations, and other **infrastructure** would have to be planned and built. However, in the years following the end of cars, the opening of these new public transportation links would make many areas much more **accessible.**

Surplus roads could be converted into tram rails to save space in city centers.

Although some people would struggle to get used to a car-free way of life, eventually many people would grow to love it! Living in accessible, greener cities would boost people's mood and mental health. People might also see their overall levels of fitness rise as they spend more time walking or bicycling.

Hi! I'm Johanna Riddle, an American scientist who studies **urban planning.** I've recently been working on a project that uses webcams to track people's facial expressions and eye movements to record their response to different city scenes. These tools can reveal hidden subconscious feelings that we aren't even aware of! Our research revealed that people are happier when looking at car-free streets than when they are looking at cars. This suggests that cars and traffic may have an important effect on our emotions, and so removing them might make people more cheerful!

A worldwide end to car sales would also have a massive impact on the global **economy.** Without any new cars to make or sell, the car **industry** would collapse. Companies that **extract,** produce, and sell gasoline and diesel would also be hit very hard, although they'd still be able to sell their products to buses, planes, and other specialist vehicles, such as tractors.

Pure elec... zero

Many places are starting to use electric buses, so **fossil fuel-** powered buses may soon become a thing of the past.

FUN FACT!

The global car industry brings in over $2.5 trillion a year!

People in car-related industries would also find themselves unemployed. Auto repair garages, car stores, and car insurance companies are just a handful of the many industries that would no longer be needed. Their employees would all lose their jobs and would have to find new careers that didn't involve cars.

However, the rise in public transportation would provide plenty of new employment opportunities. People would be needed to build, drive, and maintain new buses, trains, and trams, as well as organizing their **infrastructure.** Nationalized public transportation networks could provide extra cash for governments to make up for their lost earnings from car tax.

Car mechanics could retrain to fix buses instead.

People would also find that life without a car is much cheaper. They'd no longer need to pay for the cars themselves, gasoline, insurance, tax, maintenance, or parking, just to name a few things! This would leave them with more disposable income to save or spend on fun treats!

I ditched the car and got this awesome boat instead!

More good news

Before you read the rest of this chapter, try and think of three positive changes that aren't related to the environment that we'd see if we gave up cars.

The benefits of a car-free world don't stop with the environment ... we'd see tons of other positive changes!

Without any cars on the roads, we'd (understandably!) see a huge reduction in traffic accidents. No one would be hurt or killed in a crash. Taking cars off the road would also make it much safer to walk and bicycle around. You'd still need to watch out for buses though!

FUN FACT!

Cities that have made it much harder for people to drive cars, such as Helsinki, Finland, and Oslo, Norway, have both experienced years without a single traffic fatality!

Even without cars on the road, you'd still need to protect yourself while bicycling by wearing a helmet.

We'd also enjoy much more peace and quiet. Cars make a lot of noise, especially when they are moving quickly. Taking cars off the roads would decrease levels of noise pollution, which would improve people's mental health, sleep, and hearing. Animals would also benefit from the reduction in noise, because they'd be able to communicate more easily. This would help them escape from predators and find mates, so we might even see the populations of certain species grow as a result!

Noise pollution makes it harder for bats to find prey, because it interferes with their echolocation (the use of reflected sound to find objects).

Finally, I can find some lunch!

Can you two keep it down?!!

DID YOU KNOW?

A car traveling at 70 mph (112 kph) makes the same volume of noise as two people shouting at each other!

Our landscape has changed a lot over the past 100 years to create space for cars. Old buildings and wild areas have been cleared to build new roads, expand existing roads, and create endless parking spaces for cars. While we'd still need to keep some roads for buses and bikes, we'd definitely not need as many.

DID YOU KNOW?

In some U.S. cities, 70 percent of urban land is dedicated to parking!

By reducing the number of roads and making existing highways much narrower, we'd create loads of extra space. Some of these areas could be turned back into wild spaces by planting new native trees and plants. Eventually, animals would return to these **habitats.** Their lives would be much safer without any cars nearby!

Can you hear that? No cars, at last!

Reclaimed roads and parking lots could be used to create more **pedestrian** routes and green spaces in towns or cities. This will make it more pleasant for people to go places on foot and spend time in downtown areas. New homes and more centralized businesses could also be built on this land.

Just imagine how much more enjoyable it would be to walk by Lake Michigan in Chicago, Illinois, if the lakeside highway was an avenue for bikes and pedestrians instead!

Hi! I'm Carlos Moreno, a scientist with a particular interest in city planning. I'm very passionate about the idea of the "15-minute city," which suggests that work, stores, schools, health care, and all other daily needs should be **accessible** by a 15-minute walk, bike ride, or trip on public transit from any point in a city. Living in this type of environment would greatly improve people's quality of life.

It's 15 minutes exactly!

A simpler solution

Stopping the use of all personal cars would be a HUGE operation. It's very unlikely that it would ever happen for many reasons. For a start, carrying out a worldwide project like that would be extremely hard to organize.

Gasoline and car companies have a lot of money, and they use their wealth to lobby and convince governments not to restrict the sale of their products. It's hard to imagine that they'd allow the world to stop using cars without putting up a fight! They'd convince some countries not to cooperate, which would slow things down.

Please don't take away our money!

However, we don't need a full ban to make a difference. Some cities and countries are planning to phase out **fossil fuel-powered vehicles** over the coming years. They are investing more in public transportation and electric vehicles now, so that people can slowly get used to the change. This will make the transition much easier for everyone.

All fossil fuel-powered cars will be banned from the center of Stockholm, Sweden, from the end of 2024.

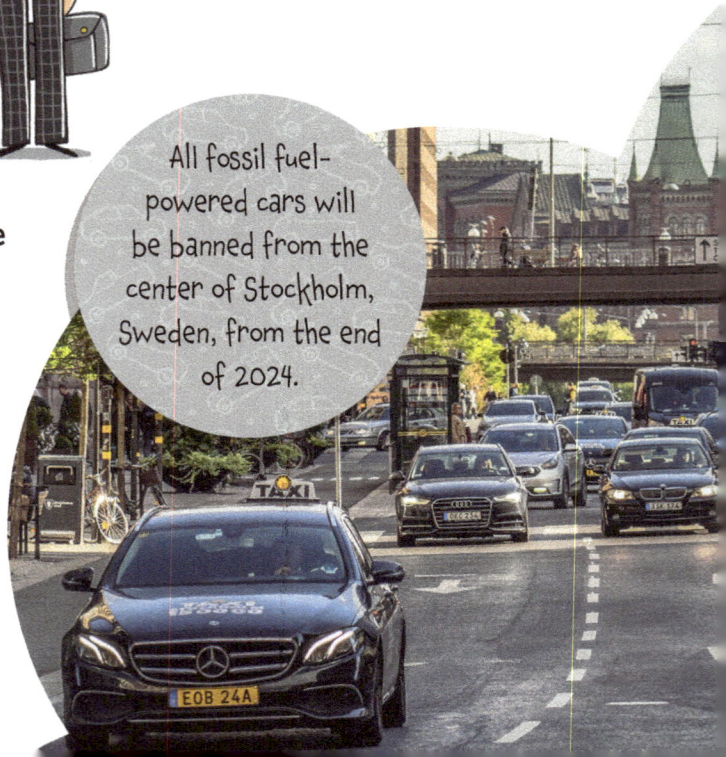

Even if countries aren't planning on banning fossil fuel-powered cars, it's still worthwhile for them to invest in their **infrastructure** so that people can depend less on cars. Improving public transit routes, building stores and key services in **accessible** areas, and installing safe sidewalks and bicycle routes will all help people leave their cars at home more often. Having better public transportation options will also benefit and improve the quality of life of those who can't drive, such as young people or people with disabilities.

Subway trains are an excellent addition to busy cities, because they provide quick and easy public transit without taking up any space on the surface!

A SIMPLER SOLUTION

There are many other things we can all do to enjoy some of the benefits of a car-free world (without actually getting rid of cars altogether!). First, an obvious one is to try and limit your use of cars as much as possible. Instead, explore other options, such as walking, bicycling, or taking public transit.

Copenhagen, Denmark, is one of the most bike-friendly cities in the world!

FUN FACT!
In Copenhagen, nearly 50 percent of trips to work or school are done on bikes!

If it's safe to walk to school where you live, why not talk to your school and see if you can set up a walking bus? This is a group of children that walks to school together along the same route every day, with adults for supervision. Setting up a walking bus might even encourage other children at your school to leave their car at home!

If you do have to use a car, make the most out of the trip! Why not set up a carpool with your friends or neighbors and travel to school together? Adults can also share rides to work. If you need to drive to run an errand, combine it with other trips so that you only need to get the car out once!

Some areas offer car-sharing schemes. If you sign up, you can reserve and use a car whenever it's available. This encourages people to only use cars when it's totally necessary and save money on car ownership, since you don't have to pay for yearly insurance or regular car maintenance.

THINK ABOUT IT!

What could you do to reduce the amount you travel by car?

Conclusion

Removing cars from our streets would have a massive positive impact on our health, our happiness, the natural world, and pretty much the entire planet! It would keep the climate crisis from getting worse, clean up our skies, and reduce many life-threatening accidents. What's not to like?!

While it's a tempting prospect, getting rid of cars altogether just isn't realistic. Too many places and people are dependent on cars, and their lives would become almost impossible without them. We also don't currently have the **infrastructure** in place to help people get around without cars, which would cause big problems.

These streets are ours now!

It's clear that we can't continue to use **fossil fuel**-powered cars as we have been. The cost to our planet is much too high, and of course, fossil fuels won't last forever! However, this change can't be made overnight. We need to start making gradual changes now to reduce our dependence on cars, so that people can transition away from them.

Some of these changes, such as investment in public transportation, need to come from governments, but many of them are things we can all do ourselves, such as walking to school or work more often.

Bus services are quick and easy to set up, and they can run on existing roads!

FUN FACT!

Riding a bike instead of driving by car saves 5.3 ounces (150 grams) of **carbon dioxide** per 0.6 miles (1 kilometer) from entering the **atmosphere**!

We'll never have a world without cars, but our world will be much healthier and more pleasant with every car we take off the roads!

Summary

So, what exactly would happen if we stopped using cars? Check your understanding of the information in this book.

We stop the use of all cars, both **fossil fuel**-powered and electric.

Air pollution drops dramatically and skies become clearer.

We see fewer health problems connected to air pollution, such as asthma, lung disease, and heart disease.

The amount of **greenhouse gases** emitted reduces, and the **greenhouse effect** stabilizes. **Climate change** doesn't get any worse.

It becomes much quieter without all that traffic noise, which benefits both humans and animals.

Phew, I'm feeling so much better now!

The car **industry** collapses and many people lose their jobs.

There are many new jobs available in the quickly growing public transportation industry. People can retrain and find a new career.

There are no more deaths from car accidents, and it becomes much safer for bicyclists and **pedestrians** on the roads.

Towns and cities change as excess roads and parking lots are reclaimed. New pedestrian areas and parks are built, making these areas much more pleasant places to live.

Many people struggle to get around in areas that don't already have public transit.

Over time, new public transit links are set up, making many places much more **accessible** than ever before.

THINK ABOUT IT!

How do you think our use of cars will have changed by the time you are an adult? What do you hope will happen?

Glossary

accessible—able to be easily reached

assembly line—a line of machines and workers in a factory that each have their own particular job

atmosphere—the blanket of gases that surrounds Earth, including nitrogen and oxygen, plus smaller amounts of such gases as carbon dioxide

carbon dioxide—a gas absorbed by plants that can contribute to global warming

climate change—changes in the world's weather, in particular, an increase in temperature, which scientists believe are mainly due to human activity

drought—a long period with little or no rain

economy—how money is made and used

emission—a release, such as giving off gas

extract—to remove

fossil fuel—a fuel such as natural gas, oil, or coal, which was formed over millions of years from the remains of animals and plants

global warming—an increase in temperatures on Earth due to the greenhouse effect

greenhouse effect—the effect caused by greenhouse gases (see below!)

greenhouse gas—a gas such as carbon dioxide or methane that gathers in the atmosphere and traps heat from the sun close to Earth's surface

habitat—the place where an animal or plant usually lives

hybrid—a hybrid car has a traditional engine powered by gasoline or diesel and a rechargeable battery

industry—the companies and activities connected to producing an item for sale or maintaining that item

infrastructure—the basic systems and services that a town, a country, or a company needs to work effectively

pedestrian—someone who is walking

remote—far away from other towns or cities

rural—in the countryside

smog—a mixture of smoke and chemicals that affects visibility and makes it hard to breathe

toxic—poisonous

urban planning—the study of how to design, build, and maintain towns and cities

Review and reflect

COMPREHENSION QUESTIONS

Driving through time

- What made cars more affordable? Why?
- Car ownership is not always a question of wealth. What are other reasons why some people do not own cars?

Our changing society

- What are some alternatives to using cars for transportation? How can the government help?
- How would a worldwide end to car sales impact the global economy?

The cost of cars

- What are some of the negative aspects about having cars?
- What are some of the challenges of life without a car?

More good news

- What would be some of the benefits of a car-free world that are not related to the environment?

Farewell cars?

- Even if we had enough fossil fuels to last forever, why shouldn't we be using them?
- What would be some of the advantages if we switched to electric cars? What would be some disadvantages?

A simpler solution

- What are some of the reasons why stopping the use of all personal cars is very unlikely?
- How can we make a difference without a full ban on cars?

A cleaner planet

- How would stopping the use of cars make a big difference to the environment?
- Why wouldn't the end of cars mean the end of global warming?

Conclusion and summary

- After reading this book and considering what would happen if we stopped using cars, what is your biggest takeaway? Why?

MAKE A CHAIN OF EVENTS!

Creating a paper chain can help you explore and visualize how cause and effect relationships can be thought of as a sequence of events.

You'll need:
- Pencil
- Scratch paper
- Pens or markers
- Stapler and staples
- Strips of paper (2 colors, if possible)

Instructions:

1. **Select a focus:** Choose a specific aspect from the book that caught your attention—it could be how your life would change if your family no longer had a car, or what would happen to animals if we no longer used cars.

2. **Brainstorm causes and effects:** On a sheet of scratch paper, brainstorm and list the causes and effects related to your chosen focus. Think critically about the factors that contributed to or resulted from your focus. You can always look back in the text for ideas!

3. **Write on strips:** Write each cause and each effect on its own strip of paper. If you have different colored paper, use one color for the cause strips and the other for the effect strips.

4. **Create the paper chain:** Organize your strips into causes and effects. Start forming a paper chain to show how a cause leads to an effect. Use the stapler to connect the two strips. Continue adding cause and effect strips as links in your chain. When you've finished, you should be able to start at the beginning of your chain and read through each chain link in a logical order.

5. **Linking multiple chains:** If your focus has multiple causes or effects, you can create additional chains and link them together to show how complex cause and effect relationships can be!

Write about it!

Look at the paper chain you created and how the causes link to effects (which in turn link to other causes!). How might breaking a link in the chain impact the overall sequence of events?

World Book, Inc.
180 North LaSalle Street
Suite 900
Chicago, Illinois 60601
USA

For information about other World Book publications, visit our website at www.worldbook.com or call 1-800-WORLDBK (967-5325).

For information about sales to schools and libraries, call 1-800-975-3250 (United States), or 1-800-837-5365 (Canada).

Library of Congress Control Number: 2024941783

What Would Happen If...
ISBN: 978-0-7166-7125-1 (set, hard cover)

We Stopped Using Cars?
ISBN: 978-0-7166-7130-5 (hard cover)
ISBN: 978-0-7166-7142-8 (e-book)
ISBN: 978-0-7166-7136-7 (soft cover)

Staff

Editorial

Vice President
Tom Evans

Editorial Project Coordinator
Kaile Kilner

Curriculum Designer
Caroline Davidson

Senior Editor
Shawn Brennan

Proofreader
Nathalie Strassheim

Graphics and Design

Senior Visual
Communications Designer
Melanie Bender

Digital Asset Specialist
Rosalia Bledsoe

Written by Izzi Howell
Illustrated by Paula Bossio

Developed with World Book
by The Dream Team

Acknowledgments

4-5   © UvGroup/Shutterstock; © Jason Benz Bennee, Shutterstock
6-7   © Shawshots/Alamy Images; © Pictorial Press Ltd/Alamy Images
8-9   © Owlie Productions/Shutterstock; © Benny Marty, Shutterstock
10-11   © Michal Vitek, Shutterstock; © Sanit Fuangnakhon, Shutterstock; © Pradeep Gaurs, Shutterstock; © FloridaStock/Shutterstock
12-13   © Jed RT/Shutterstock; © Robert Crum, Shutterstock
14-15   © Pandora Pictures/Shutterstock
16-17   © J.J. Gouin, Shutterstock; © Red ivory/Shutterstock
18-19   © Schroptschop/iStock; © Sunart Media/Shutterstock
20-21   © MyCreative/Shutterstock; © Cynthia Lee, Alamy Images; © Monkey Business Images/Shutterstock
22-23   © potowizard/Shutterstock; © Sk Hasan Ali/Shutterstock
26-27   © Lena Platonova, Shutterstock; © kdshutterman/ Shutterstock
28-29   © Markus Mainka, Shutterstock; © Sahara Prince, Shutterstock
30-31   © Nastasic/iStock; © Xinhua/Alamy Images
32-33   © Edwin Tan, iStock; © Rudmer Zwerver, Shutterstock
34-35   © Jaysi/iStock; © stockphoto mania/Shutterstock
36-37   © Dmitry Kalinovsky, Shutterstock; © George Clerk, iStock
38-39   © sevenke/Shutterstock; © Michele Ursi, Shutterstock
40-41   © Monkey Business Images/Shutterstock; © John T, Shutterstock

www.ingramcontent.com/pod-product-compliance
Lightning Source LLC
Chambersburg PA
CBHW060858090426
42737CB00023B/3484